Ancient Inscriptions:
SIDELIGHTS ON GREEK HISTORY

*Three Lectures on the Light thrown
by Greek Inscriptions on the Life
and Thought of the Ancient World*

By MARCUS N. TOD, M.A., F.B.A.
*Fellow and Tutor of Oriel College, Oxford,
and University Reader in Greek Epigraphy*

ARES PUBLISHERS INC.
CHICAGO MCMLXXIV

Unchanged Reprint of the Edition:
Oxford, 1932.
ARES PUBLISHERS INC.
150 E. Huron Street
Chicago, Illinois 60611
Printed in the United States of America
International Standard Book Number:
0-89005-039-2
Library of Congress Catalog Card Number:
74-77896

PREFACE

WHEN the Academic Council of the University of London honoured me with an invitation to deliver a course of three lectures on some subject connected with the Classics, it expressed a hope that the lectures so given might subsequently be published. This will, I hope, serve as a sufficient justification for offering this little book to a wider audience than that which heard its contents at University College on 26th February and 5th and 12th March, 1931. They appear here almost word for word as they were then spoken, for I have felt that little, if any, advantage was to be gained by divesting them of the traits which are natural in lectures and substituting those more appropriate to a book. In any case, I trust that those readers who feel (and none can feel more acutely than I) the inadequacy of the discussion afforded in the following pages to the subjects with which they deal will by the very form of treatment be reminded of the inevitable limitations under which a lecturer suffers.

A few notes are added at the close of each lecture to enable students who are so minded to follow up for themselves the lines of thought suggested in the text.

M. N. T.

CONTENTS

		page
I.	The Characteristics and Value of the Evidence derived from Inscriptions	11
II.	Inter-state Arbitration in the Greek World	39
III.	Clubs and Societies in the Greek World	71

ABBREVIATIONS

B.C.H. = *Bulletin de Correspondance Hellénique.*

C.I.L. = *Corpus Inscriptionum Latinarum.*

Cl. Qu. = *Classical Quarterly.*

I.G. = *Inscriptiones Graecae.*

J.H.S. = *Journal of Hellenic Studies.*

J.R.S. = *Journal of Roman Studies.*

O.G.I. = Dittenberger, *Orientis Graeci Inscriptiones Selectae.*

Rev. Phil. = *Revue de Philologie.*

R.É.G. = *Revue des Études Grecques.*

S.E.G. = *Supplementum Epigraphicum Graecum.*

S.I.G. = Dittenberger, *Sylloge Inscriptionum Graecarum* (3rd edition).

LECTURE I

THE CHARACTERISTICS AND VALUE OF THE EVIDENCE DERIVED FROM INSCRIPTIONS

LECTURE I

The Characteristics and Value of the Evidence derived from Inscriptions

IT is no part of my task in this lecture to summarize or to estimate the additions made by inscriptions to our knowledge of ancient life. To make any such attempt would be to court certain failure. For there is no part of the Greek world, no period of Greek history, no aspect of Greek thought and activity on which Greek inscriptions have not thrown fresh and valuable light. The debt which we, as students of the ancient world, owe to the epigraphical evidence is so great, and increases so rapidly with the progress of excavation and exploration, of decipherment and interpretation, that to appraise it adequately would demand a survey of the ancient world from the beginning of the classical period down to the dawn of the Middle Ages. Moreover, it is an impossible task to discriminate satisfactorily between the knowledge derived from our literary sources and that due to inscriptions, so intricately do the two classes of evidence dovetail into each other, each of them confirming or correcting, modifying or supplementing, the conclusions we should draw from the other. My own task this evening is the much humbler one of calling your attention to some of the outstanding characteristics of the epigraphical evidence, and especially to those which differentiate it to some degree from that afforded by ancient literature, giving only such few illustrations as the narrow limits of a single lecture will permit, and at the same time to point out some of the fields in which the inscriptions are of the greatest value to us. In other words, I shall seek to show rather the nature than the extent and content of the contribution of inscriptions to our knowledge of the Greek world. In the two following lectures I shall deal with two particular topics, one drawn from the public and the other from the private life of the Greeks, and seek, while indicating some of the main conclusions which may be drawn from our epigraphical evidence, to illustrate still further the salient features of those materials.

To me it seems that one of the most interesting experiences attending the advanced study of the classics is that of the ever-broadening horizons which open out before us, of the increasing variety of the materials out of which the edifice of our knowledge is to be erected, or, if I may change the metaphor, the number and variety of the allies on whom we may call for assistance in our quest. At the outset we accepted what we were told about Greek life and history, almost without question. It was the business of the teacher who instructed us, of the author whose work we studied, to know what people were like and what they did; whence that knowledge was derived we hardly stopped to ask. Our task was to understand, or at least to remember, what we were told. At the next stage, when we began to become more familiar with the classical literature, we realized the source from which was derived much (at first we were, maybe, inclined to think all) of our knowledge of ancient history. Later, however, in our last days at school and still more at the University, our outlook still further expands. The resources of geography and geology, of hydrography and meteorology are laid under contribution in order that we may the better understand the physical features of that world in which the drama of Greek history was played, and the material conditions under which the lives of the actors were lived.[1] At first, perhaps, this appears to us primarily a question of fitness : we want to see before our mental vision the personalities and the actions of the ancient world against their suitable, that is their historical, background, to realize them not *in vacuo* but in their true physical environment. But it is not long before we take a further step and perceive that geography gives us no mere background, however picturesque and appropriate, but a vital factor, helping to make persons and events what they are. For geographical surroundings do not merely witness the development of national character and achievement ; to some extent they determine them. Archaeology, again, has in countless ways contributed to the better understanding of Greek life.[2] It has unearthed, studied and interpreted the material relics of Hellenic civilization, the remains of temples and walls, of houses and tombs, and the lesser works, whether of utility or of beauty, created by the hand of man—his arms, furniture, utensils, vases and ornaments. From these we learn much, in conjunction with the literary evidence, of topography, much also of the way in which the Greeks lived, of the objects with which they surrounded themselves, of the buildings which witnessed their public and social activities and their religious observances, and of the development alike of their craftsmanship and of their aesthetic sense. At the same time archaeology affords us countless pictures, both engraved in stone and painted on earthenware, illustrating various aspects of Greek practice and belief. Anthropology brings to us its accumulated store of observation and reflection,[3] enabling us to understand much that might otherwise be obscure in the customs of the Greeks and to trace affinities, alike physical and spiritual, between them and other races, while philology performs a somewhat similar task in the realm of language. Papyrology has, during the past half-century, immeasurably enriched our knowledge of antiquity, not only by the additions which it has made to classical and post-classical literature but also by the intense light which it has thrown upon the organization and the life of Ptolemaic and of Greco-Roman

Egypt, especially upon those aspects of them which do not readily lend themselves to literary treatment. The study of numismatics, too, working upon materials lying midway between the archaeological and the epigraphical, has proved an invaluable aid, —mainly, but not solely, in the fields of economics and of chronology.[4]

But of these I must not speak further, for I wish to concentrate your attention upon one member of this goodly band of allies and to consider what services he is best fitted to render.

The utilization of inscriptions as historical documents has a long history.[5] Clear traces of it are found in the works of Herodotus and Thucydides and of most, if not all, of their chief successors in the field of historiography. The orators frequently appeal to epigraphical evidence to corroborate their statements, and the first half of the third century B.C. witnessed the publication of two works which were largely or wholly epigraphical, Philochorus' ἐπιγράμματα Ἀττικά and the ψηφισμάτων συναγωγή of Craterus the Macedonian, half-brother of Antigonus Gonatas, a notable work consisting of at least nine books and dominated throughout by a historical aim and interest. Cyriac of Ancona, merchant and dilettante, copied so large a number of inscriptions, both Greek and Latin, in the course of his travels in the first half of the fifteenth century that he has been called the father of modern Greek epigraphy. The second half of that century as well as the two centuries which followed were marked by the publication of numerous collections of inscriptions, for the most part Latin rather than Greek. The eighteenth century rendered the Greek world more accessible to foreign scholars and the number of known Greek inscriptions was rapidly increased by the labours of Fourmont, Chishull, Chandler, Choiseul-Gouffier and others, followed in the early part of last century by Leake, Dodwell, Rose, Osann, Letronne and other scholars.

A new era dawned when the publication of a *corpus* of all known Greek inscriptions, projected by Maffei as early as 1732, was undertaken in 1815 by the Prussian Academy. August Böckh was put in charge of the enterprise. No choice could have been more fortunate: Böckh combined in a remarkable degree genius, learning and industry, and all of these he devoted unsparingly to the exacting task. The first fascicule of the great *Corpus Inscriptionum Graecarum* appeared in 1825, and the work was brought to a conclusion in 1877, ten years after the death of Böckh and twenty-six after that of Franz, his principal collaborator, by Ernst Curtius, Adolf Kirchhoff and others. Thus was well and truly laid the foundation of the modern scientific study of Greek inscriptions,—a complete, critical edition of all the epigraphical texts already known, carried out with admirable determination by a group of great scholars. Nevertheless the work was, in a certain sense, out of date as soon as it was published. The successful issue of the Greek War of Liberation stimulated the exploration of the country and the careful study of all the surviving remains of antiquity, among which inscriptions took a prominent place. Then followed the era of systematic excavation of ancient sites, which has resulted in the discovery of tens of thousands of inscriptions. A new *Corpus* was imperatively demanded, and once again the Berlin Academy sponsored the work, undertaking the publication of all inscriptions found within the confines of Europe. The year 1873, four years before that in which the enterprise launched in 1815 was completed, witnessed the publication of the first volume of the new collection (which bears the title *Inscriptiones Graecae* to distinguish it from the older *Corpus Inscriptionum Graecarum*), Kirchhoff's masterly edition of the Attic inscriptions prior to 403 B.C. For full fifty years this volume proved an invaluable aid to the study of Athenian history during its most brilliant period, nor is it entirely superseded even now, although a second edition, published in 1924 and garnering the fruits of half a century of excavation and investigation, has for most purposes taken its place. Meanwhile the colossal enterprise has progressed apace, though we can hardly yet claim that its completion is within sight; the Vienna Academy has made, and in part fulfilled, a promise to deal similarly with the inscriptions of Asia Minor; the first part of a *corpus* of Greek and Latin inscriptions of Syria appeared in 1929, and preparations are going forward for a complete collection of the Greek inscriptions discovered in Egypt.

Meanwhile, side by side with these comprehensive collections, we have a number of selections of epigraphical texts chosen for their special interest or as the representatives of important categories. Among these, three demand special mention, Dittenberger's *Sylloge Inscriptionum Graecarum*, now in its third edition, Michel's *Recueil d'Inscriptions Grecques* and Roberts and Gardner's *Introduction to Greek Epigraphy*, ii., an admirable selection of 410 Attic inscriptions of every type and period, accompanied by a helpful commentary in English.

Yet, despite these and countless other aids, it cannot be maintained that the study of Greek inscriptions is an easy one. Their number is almost overwhelmingly great and is constantly and rapidly increasing. When Böckh undertook his great task he appraised at about 6000 the number of known Greek inscriptions; now I imagine that 75,000 would be a conservative estimate. In Böckh's *Corpus*, for example, there are sixteen inscriptions from Epidaurus, but by 1929 these had increased to 745[6]; from Arcadia Böckh knew but thirty, while in 1913 Hiller von Gaertringen collected 565 in the Arcadian volume of the *Inscriptiones Graecae*.[7] Nor are we confronted solely by the numerical increase of our materials. Inscriptions already known are more closely studied, more accurately deciphered, more correctly restored, more adequately interpreted. New discoveries demand the reconsideration of accepted conclusions, and theories apparently justified to-day may have to be modified or even abandoned to-morrow. Progress is incessant; finality seems unattainable. And this work is carried on by scholars in a score of countries and is published in over a dozen languages in a bewildering number of books, dissertations and periodicals. These difficulties I emphasize, not to discourage but to stimulate you. They are not peculiar to the study of Greek epigraphy, but confront the serious student of every important subject, whether in the humanistic sphere or in that of the natural sciences. And they are surely the consequences, and thus the guarantees, of the fact that this study is one which excites a widespread and vivid interest, and that it is essentially progressive and not stagnant. In my own case at least it has exercised a strong and ever-growing fascination since first I approached it as a novice almost thirty years ago.

But, it may well be asked, are Greek inscriptions anything more than fragments of Greek writings, for the most part admittedly destitute of literary style and beauty, which happen to owe their survival to stone or bronze rather than to vellum or papyrus ? are they not the flotsam and jetsam cast up upon the shores of modern times by the caprice of the sea which has engulfed so much of the ancient world ? are not most of them seriously mutilated or, even if complete, lacking in historical value ? is not our time better spent upon the masterpieces of historical literature, such as the works of Herodotus, Thucydides and Polybius, or at least upon continuous and intelligible narratives, such as those of Xenophon, Diodorus or Plutarch ? have not even the fragments of the Greek poets and historians a prior claim on us ? had we not better leave inscriptions to the few specialists who apparently enjoy the requisite leisure and whose idiosyncrasy leads them into this by-path of study ?

With this attitude and these questionings I should like to deal sympathetically, and to acknowledge fully their *prima facie* justification.

It is true that our epigraphical texts, and especially the longer and more valuable ones, are in many cases mutilated. A prolonged exposure to the weather may have rendered much of them illegible, or, like a recently discovered recital of the marvels wrought by Asclepius at his sanctuary near Epidaurus,[8] they may have served as threshold-stones and been worn away by the feet of many generations. Others, again, have been broken, either by accident or deliberately, and of the fragments some have irretrievably perished. Of the dramatic *didascaliae* from Athens, for example, a document of incalculable value for the history of the Attic drama, fourteen fragments have been recovered containing the whole or part of fewer than two hundred lines out of the eight or nine thousand which, it has been calculated, originally composed the record.[9] Of an Attic inscription containing the accounts of state loans for 426-5 to 423-2 B.C. and the interest due thereon, ably reconstructed in a recent work by Dr. B. D. Meritt,[10] fifteen fragments survive, yet they constitute less than a half of the original text, while of the re-assessment of the tribute of the Athenian Empire in 425-4 B.C. we possess a much larger number of fragments but probably a smaller proportion of the whole text.[11] Much, it is true, may be done by scientific restoration to minimize the losses so sustained, for the close adherence of public documents to stereotyped formulae greatly facilitates the restoration of mutilated passages; yet despite every effort many inscriptions baffle all attempts to restore their content convincingly, and sometimes the portion which is missing is essential for the dating or the interpretation of the document as a whole.

Yet while all this is unquestionable, we must bear in mind that it is not true of inscriptions alone but of a large part of the rich inheritance which antiquity has bequeathed to us. The very Parthenon is but a shell, shattered by the explosion of a Turkish powder-magazine; the exquisite Nike-temple has been reconstructed from fragments collected from the great Frankish tower which for centuries occupied its site. How many of the temples and palaces, the walls and towers of ancient Greece survive intact ? how many of the extant masterpieces of Greek sculpture are undamaged ? Is not the same true even of Greek literature ? Look at the literary fragments among the Oxyrhynchus papyri. Remember how few among the dramas even of Aeschylus, Sophocles and Euripides we possess entire. Realize how much of Polybius and Diodorus has perished. Turn the pages of the *Fragmenta Tragicorum*, the *Fragmenta Comicorum*, the *Fragmenta Historicorum*, and they will tell the same tale, that, while some works of antiquity have come down to us unimpaired, we stand amid the shattered fragments of a bygone world. Better value and appreciate what we have than pine for what is lost ; better extract by careful decipherment, close study, cautious and scientific restoration, all that is of interest in what still survives than neglect it because there is so much more for which we long.

Again, we must frankly acknowledge the disconnected character of the inscriptions. Just as the stones on which they survive are physically isolated units, so each inscription tells us, in the great majority of cases, a separate story, or, if there is any continuity between them, it is generally the continuity of chance rather than of design. There are, it is true, exceptions. The " Parian Marble,"[12] for example, contains a chronological list of the outstanding events in Greek history, each precisely dated, from the accession of Cecrops in 1582 B.C. down to 263 B.C., when the list was inscribed. We possess, again, by far the greater part of a list[13] of Milesian eponymous magistrates extending from 525 B.C. to A.D. 31, as well as a list[14] of those who had held the priesthood of Poseidon at Halicarnassus, recording not only their names but the number of years during which each was in office, beginning with Poseidon's son Telamon and extending down to about 100 B.C. These, however, are exceptional and not typical. Normally each inscription records one event, it contains one law or decree or the accounts of a single building, it marks one dedication or commemorates one death or the deaths of those who fell in a common enterprise. But the framework of our knowledge, the continuous historical narrative, the summaries of characters, periods or movements which give us broad vistas,—these we owe almost wholly to our literary sources. To write a history of Greece from literary evidence alone is a possible undertaking, though I should be sorry to embark upon it : Mitford and Thirlwall achieved it and the same might be said, with but little qualification, of Grote. But who can imagine a history of Greece based wholly upon inscriptions ? It would lack an intelligible and coherent framework, for many even of the inscriptions which are of the greatest value would lose much of their importance and interest were it not for the light thrown on them by literature. The illumination afforded by a literary record is often dim and diffused. A situation, a policy, a character, an age may be summed up in a phrase. We see the outlines only, the salient facts, but little or no detail. Inscriptions rarely diffuse their light: they illuminate vividly, intensely, one small spot, leaving all around in darkness.

Once more, as we study the inscriptions, we realize that no process of natural selection has been at work determining their preservation, that there has been no tendency for the most valuable to survive. This is especially clear when we look at the *corpora*, or complete collections, rather than at the selections in which the most interesting documents alone are reproduced and the remainder are ignored. How worthless many of the extant fragments appear, mutilated beyond hope of restoration or interpretation (though growing experience will make us hesitate more and more to dismiss any of them as valueless), dedications or epitaphs of men or women unknown to history, boundary-stones uprooted ages ago from the spots at which alone they had their true significance ! How capricious, how ruthless fortune has been ! Contrast the conditions under which much of our classical literature has survived. Sometimes, it is true, the preservation of some work

Sidelights on Greek History 25

seems due to a freak of chance, and here too, whether on fragments of papyrus or in the citations of later authors, grammarians or lexicographers, countless fragments survive which have little or no historical or literary value. But in general we may say that works tended to survive because of their intrinsic merit, because they were judged worthy of immortality, because they enjoyed the largest circulation and therefore had the greatest chance of survival. In the epigraphical realm no analogous process of selection has been operative. Of each inscribed text there was normally but one example. If this was destroyed, the writing engraved upon it was lost for ever, for the ancient selections of inscriptions made by Philochorus and Craterus have perished.

But granted that we admit, and even emphasize, these defects, are we justified in neglecting the epigraphical evidence ? A full reply would demand a longer time than that now at my disposal, but I shall suggest a few lines of thought in the hope that you may follow them up at your leisure.

Bear in mind, then, that we are not confronted by the alternative, literature *or* inscriptions. The two are not mutually exclusive, but inextricably intertwined ; they are not jealous foes, but sworn allies. Never, I hope, has my enthusiasm for inscriptions led me to speak a word derogatory to Greek literature, which, in my judgement, is, and must always remain, of supreme value in the study of Greek history. But surely those who are most fascinated by that literature, most responsive to its appeal, should be the first to welcome the fresh knowledge that comes from inscriptions and throws new and valuable light alike upon the form and upon the content of that literature. So far as our literary and epigraphical sources are true, they cannot be ultimately inconsistent, though they may be mutually complementary, and we who profess to seek after an understanding of the life and thought of the ancient world must, if we are in earnest, pursue our quest by every available avenue, so that our knowledge may be as full, as exact, as comprehensive as we can make it.

Let me add one or two illustrations drawn from the field in which I am more particularly interested, Greek History. Even when we possess the complete narrative of a historian, however competent, inscriptions may be of value in confirming or supplementing or, rarely, correcting it. Thucydides gives us (V. 47) the text of the quadruple alliance of 420 B.C. between Athens, Argos, Elis and Mantinea. Part of the Attic stele bearing the terms of this alliance has come to light, strikingly confirming the historian's accuracy, yet showing us what liberties he allowed himself in view of the fact that his work, as revised for publication, would contain only a summary of the terms of the alliance and not its full text. Even

Sidelights on Greek History 27

where Thucydides' narrative is fairly detailed, as in his story of the Samian War of 440 and 439, inscriptions add considerably to our knowledge and give us a far more adequate understanding of the widespread disaffection and of the precarious condition of the Athenian Empire at that crisis, as well as of the terms granted to Samos after its capitulation. Again, it is from inscriptions only that we derive any knowledge of some of the most important events of the period covered by Thucydides, such as the startling increase of the Attic tribute by the assessment of 425–4 B.C. and the measures taken by the Athenians to impose upon all their allies the use of Attic currency, weights and measures.[15]

Nor must we forget that inscriptions do much more than merely dot the i's and cross the t's of our literary evidence. We owe to them alone certain documents, the interest of which for the study of Greek literature and ancient history it would be hard to overrate. A long catalogue could easily be drawn up, but I must content myself here with a few examples : your own knowledge will readily suggest others. In the field of Greek poetry we may note the long hymn of Isis discovered at Andros (to which fresh attention has recently been drawn by a prose version of the same theme which has come to light at Cyme[16]), the poems of Isyllus and Maiistas, the Hymn of the Curetes, the paeans of the Athenian Limenius and the Locrian Philodamus and other poetical works collected in J. U. Powell's *Collectanea Alexandrina*; in that of the history of literature I may again refer to the fragments of the dramatic *didascaliae* and of the cognate *fasti* and victor-lists.[17] For philosophy the long, but unhappily mutilated, *dossier* in which Diogenes of Oenoanda sought to explain and establish his Epicurean faith is of no little interest.[18] The student of ancient law possesses in the fifth-century Code of Gortyn a document of unique value,[19] while the constitution of the Hellenic League founded in 302 B.C. by Antigonus Monophthalmus and Demetrius Poliorcetes[20] as a renewal of the earlier Corinthian League of Philip and Alexander, and the revised constitution of Cyrene,[21] about the dating of which scholars are still at variance, give to the constitutional historian detailed data such as the literary tradition rarely affords. The " Parian Marble " is by far the earliest chronological record of its kind. For Roman history also Greek inscriptions have conserved materials of great value. The five perfectly preserved decrees of Augustus recently unearthed at Cyrene[22] add considerably to our knowledge of the policy of the founder of the Principate and his intervention in public provinces of the Empire, while his official autobiography, the *Res gestae divi Augusti*, is widely known as the *Monumentum Ancyranum* from its discovery, alike in the original Latin and in a Greek translation, among the ruins of the temple of Roma and Augustus at Ancyra, the capital of Galatia.[23] For the economic historian as well as for the lexicographer the Edict of Diocletian, issued in A.D. 301 and published in Latin and in Greek throughout the eastern provinces of the Empire, supplies materials unparalleled elsewhere.[24] It was designed to check profiteering by fixing the maxima which could legally be demanded for all commodities and all services: these maxima are calculated in copper *denarii* and since the price of pure gold is preserved, we can calculate the absolute as well as the comparative values prescribed.

But it is not mainly, still less solely, on the ground of such outstanding epigraphical documents that we base our estimate of the value of inscriptions. There are problems, or even whole fields, of Greek language, thought and life, in which they constitute our sole, or at least our main, sources. The derivation and development of Greek writing, the vocabulary, spelling or grammar of a given area or period, the characteristics of dialects represented inadequately, if at all, in our extant literature,—these and similar inquiries owe to inscriptions vast masses of evidence of unquestionable authenticity. Or, turning from language to history, what should we know of the membership, organization and resources of the Athenian Empire but for the contemporary decrees, quota-lists[25] and assessments? or of the administration and composition of the Athenian navy but for the long and elaborate navy-lists[26]? The manumission of slaves and the position of freedmen are illustrated by hundreds of emancipation-records preserved at Delphi and elsewhere. Of two further subjects, the application of arbitral methods to the settlement of inter-state disputes and the activities of the Greek associations, I shall say something in the two following lectures. Historians tend to tell of the abnormal,—of wars and revolutions, of disasters and of events which owe their interest largely to their singularity. Inscriptions also tell of these things, but not primarily, much less exclusively. To them we must turn for a picture of normal life,—its work, its play, its education, its family life, its religious observances. Through them we must approach, if at all, the common people who form so large a proportion of every community. Here, in masses of texts not specially selected to prove any theory, we shall find materials for generalizations and means of understanding the ordinary man. Literature will tell us, for example, of the attitude of Socrates or of Seneca to death: but to learn how the average Greek regarded it, we must turn to the countless epitaphs of men and women unknown to fame, in which we find set forth, often in faulty spelling and grammar and metre, the thoughts which death inspired. If what we seek is a history of princes, of statesmen, of warriors, inscriptions may possibly disappoint us: if we wish to interpret the life and aims of the people, we shall find in them a rich and inexhaustible treasure-house.

Three further characteristics of the inscriptions call for mention before I close this survey.

They are, in almost every case, contemporary with the events which they record, and so are unaffected by any knowledge of subsequent occurrences, any distortion of perspective, any risk of anachronism. How little of our historical literature is contemporary in this full sense ! Even for Thucydides we cannot make this claim, for his story of the Peloponnesian War bears clear traces of having been revised after, and in the light of, its conclusion. No work, perhaps, could pass the test save one written and published as a diary. I am not exalting inscriptions at the expense of history : I am only calling attention to one of the differences between them. I do not deny that history often gains by being written after an interval : the proportions are better realized, the emotions of the moment have subsided, acts are more justly appraised because their developments and effects can be to some extent traced. Yet the historian must, if possible, frequently have recourse to evidence which dates from the period with which he is dealing, in order that he may see the hard, precise facts of history as they appeared to the contemporary view. Such materials the inscriptions constantly supply. A corollary of this may be found in the first-hand nature of our epigraphical records. Writers frequently draw upon various sources, disparate in character and various in value. Traditions become coloured or even radically altered by the lapse of time or under the influence of interest, prejudice, misconception or forgetfulness. Many, if not most, reach us at second or third hand, and their original forms, the exact truth underlying historical traditions, may be hard or impossible to recover. Inscriptions give us not tradition but fact; they were stereotyped, so to say, on the day on which they came into being. Rarely—I would not say never—are we in our study of them confronted with problems of *Quellenforschung*.

And with this quality goes another of yet greater importance, the objectivity of the epigraphical sources and their freedom from bias. In the study of ancient literature we are frequently bidden to examine the so-called " personal factor," to determine the predilections and prejudices of writers or of their sources, and to make the requisite adjustments in the pictures they present. The study of inscriptions hardly ever involves any such process, for these embody facts rather than judgements, they register deeds rather thau examine motives. If the writings of many Greek authors pulsate with the throb of the intense and sometimes bitter personal or family or party feeling natural to the Greek temperament and fostered by the peculiar conditions of the city-state, the epigraphical records are normally as cold and unmoved as the stones on which they are engraved.

I close by drawing attention to what is perhaps the outstanding feature of inscriptions, their detailed character. Historians constantly, and rightly, use round numbers. The Boeotians at Delium, Thucydides says, numbered " about 7000 heavy infantry, over 10,000 light troops, 1000 cavalry and 500 peltasts[27] "; the siege of Potidaea cost " 2000 talents[28] "; the coined silver on the Acropolis in 431 was worth "6000 talents," the uncoined gold and silver " at least 500 talents[29]." Such approximations are wholly alien to inscriptions, which give exact figures and are as scrupulous about an obol as about a talent. The historian, again, sums up a law, a treaty, a decree in a sentence, omitting all or most of its details; an inscription records every word, every letter of such a document. The very fact that in Book V. Thucydides quotes several treaties *in extenso* has been regarded (rightly, I think) as indicating that the historian never revised this book and prepared it for publication.[30] The writer of history frequently contents himself with recording results; inscriptions enable us to understand the working of the machinery as well as to examine its product in detail. Hence we gain greatly in precision and exactitude: bare outlines are enriched with interesting and significant details. Moreover, by giving us wholly objective and authoritative accounts of certain historical events which our literary sources also record, epigraphy enables us to determine more accurately the credibility of those sources and the methods of their authors.

Let it not be objected that these details are trivial. The edifice of knowledge is built not alone of massive blocks but also of small stones, and it is surprising how often some trifling fact helps us to grasp better some important character or situation, and how scattered fragments, each valueless in isolation, can be correlated so as to yield results of striking and permanent value. The whole vast business of modern insurance, for example, rests upon averages derived from the accumulation of facts individually insignificant.

These, then, are some of the main characteristics, as I conceive them, of inscriptions regarded as evidence for ancient life. I have sought to be fair, to avoid exaggeration, to say no work of disparagement of the other categories of evidence which are available. But I hope to have created, or rather confirmed, the conviction that inscriptions have no unimportant part to play in the interpretation of the ancient world, and that the time and labour which their close study demands is likely to be richly rewarded.

NOTES ON LECTURE I

[1] Cf., e.g., A. E. Zimmern, *The Greek Commonwealth*, Part i. ; J. L. Myres, *Greek Lands and the Greek People*.

[2] Cf., e.g., M. Cary, *Documentary Sources of Greek History*, ch. x. ; P. Gardner, *New Chapters in Greek History* ; E. A. Gardner in D. G. Hogarth, *Authority and Archaeology*, Part ii., ch. iii.

[3] Cf. *Anthropology and the Classics*, edited by R. R. Marett.

[4] Cf. M. Cary, *op. cit.*, ch. ix. ; P. Gardner, *History of Ancient Coinage*; G. F. Hill, *Historical Greek Coins*; J. G. Milne, *Greek Coinage*.

[5] S. Chabert, *Histoire sommaire des études d'épigraphie grecque* ; W. Larfeld, *Griechische Epigraphik*[3], 7ff.

[6] *I.G.* iv.[2] 1, edited by F. Hiller von Gaertringen.

[7] *I.G.* v. 2.

[8] *I.G.* iv.[2] 1. 123.

[9] A. Wilhelm, *Urkunden dramatischer Aufführungen in Athen*, 34ff.

[10] *The Athenian Calendar in the fifth Century*.

[11] *I.G.* i.[2] 63. Cf. *J.H.S.* xlvii. 186.

[12] *I.G.* xii. 5. 444. The best edition is F. Jacoby, *Das Marmor Parium*.

[13] *Milet*, i. 3, *Das Delphinion in Milet*, 122–8.

[14] *S.I.G.* 1020.

[15] *S.I.G.* 87 ; cf. P. Gardner, *op. cit.* 226ff.

[16] *I.G.* xii. 5. 739 (cf. *ibid.* 14 and p. 217) ; A. Salač, *B.C.H.* li., 378 ff., P. Roussel, *R.É.G.* xlii. 137 ff. Cf. W. Peek, *Der Isishymnus von Andros.*

[17] A. Wilhelm, *op. cit.*, A. E. Haigh, *The Attic Theatre*[3], 352 ff., *S.I.G.* 1078, *I.G.* ii.[2] 2318-25.

[18] *Diogenis Oenoandensis Fragmenta*, ed. J. William.

[19] Hicks and Hill, *Greek Hist. Inscr.* 35, Dareste, Haussoulier et Reinach, *Recueil des inscriptions juridiques grecques*, i. 352 ff., J. Kohler und E. Ziebarth, *Das Stadtrecht von Gortyn*, Göttingen, 1912.

[20] *I.G.* iv.[2] 1. 68 ; cf. W. W. Tarn, *J.H.S.* xlii. 198 ff.

[21] *Rivista di filologia classica*, N.S. vi. 183 ff.; cf. M. Cary, *J.H.S.* xlviii. 222 ff. For a fuller bibliography see *J.H.S.* xlvii. 216, xlix. 214.

[22] *Rivista di filologia classica*, N.S. vi. 321 ff.; cf. J. G. C. Anderson, *J.R.S.* xvii. 33 ff. For a fuller bibliography see *J.H.S.* xlix. 215.

[23] E. G. Hardy, *The Monumentum Ancyranum*, Oxford, 1923, E. Diehl, *Res gestae Divi Augusti.*

[24] *C.I.L.* iii., p. 1926 ff., 2208 ff., 2328[57] ff.; T. Mommsen und H. Blümner, *Der Maximaltarif des Diocletian.*

[25] For the remarkable work recently accomplished in the restoration of these lists by A. B. West and B. D. Meritt see *J.H.S.* xlvii. 187 ff., xlix. 181 f. Their final readings of the quota-lists have appeared in *S.E.G.* v.

[26] *I.G.* ii². 1604 ff.

[27] Thuc. iv. 93. 3.

[28] Thuc. ii. 70. 2.

[29] Thuc. ii. 13. 3, 4.

[30] J. B. Bury, *Ancient Greek Historians*, 85.

LECTURE II

INTER-STATE ARBITRATION IN THE GREEK WORLD

LECTURE II

INTER-STATE ARBITRATION IN THE GREEK WORLD

IN my previous lecture I called your attention to some of the outstanding features of the evidence for ancient thought and life which we derive from Greek inscriptions, and especially to those which differentiate that evidence from the historical and literary works more familiar to most of us. To-day I shall deal with the subject of inter-state arbitration in the Greek world, partly on account of its intrinsic interest and importance, partly because in this study the value of the epigraphical materials and their peculiar characteristics will, I hope, find fuller and clearer illustration.

The question is one which has excited some interest, especially since its treatment by Erich Sonne in his dissertation *De arbitris externis* (Göttingen, 1888). The brilliant French scholar and publicist, Victor Bérard, chose it as the subject of his thesis[1] in 1894, and Coleman Phillipson devoted a chapter to it in his valuable work entitled *The International Law and Custom of Ancient Greece and Rome*, published in 1911. In 1912 an exhaustive study in French, from the pen of A. Raeder, was issued under the auspices of the Norwegian Nobel Institute,[2] and in the following year I published a shorter essay[3] on the same theme, completed before the appearance of

Raeder's work. Since then no comprehensive treatment of the subject has been undertaken, despite the considerable accessions made to our knowledge in the course of the last eighteen years and the enormous impetus given to the study by the tragic events of the great war and the consequent efforts, fostered principally by the League of Nations, to substitute arbitration for war in the solution of international differences. I have reason, however, to believe that the publication of a *corpus* of the Greek evidence, with translation and historical commentary, is contemplated.

I shall not attempt in this lecture to give a complete survey of the subject, but shall content myself with answering in outline some of the questions which are likely to suggest themselves to your minds, and with pointing out how valuable is the light shed by inscriptions upon every aspect of the subject, but more especially upon that which our literary sources almost entirely ignore, the precise method and machinery by which the arbitral process was carried out.

But first let me say a few words in general about the attitude of the Greeks to war.[4] The first impression made upon our minds by the study of Greek literature, and more particularly of historical literature, is that the Greek world was the scene of almost unbroken strife. The *Iliad* rings throughout with the clash of arms; the lyric poets sing the praises of martial valour and urge their fellow-citizens to war; Herodotus selects as his theme the conflict between Hellenism and the "barbarian" East, culminating in the repulse of Xerxes' invasion, and Thucydides narrates the life-and-death struggle between the leading powers of Hellas. In Xenophon's *Hellenica*, too, war plays a sadly dominant part, and even the triumph of the Macedonian monarchs brings little or no respite. Greek independence is crushed that Greek forces may be employed in Alexander's grand crusade, and after his death the Greek world is rent by the struggles of his successors and, later, by those of the Greek Leagues, until at length the *Pax Romana* comes to a world worn out by strife, depopulated and impoverished,—the peace of exhaustion, if not of death.

Yet is this first impression wholly true? Beside the *Iliad* stand the *Odyssey*, the Homeric Hymns and Hesiod's song of husbandry. Among the lyric poets are some who find no thrill or glamour in war, who in its place exalt faithfulness, honour, love and " the glorious gifts of the Muses and Aphrodite." Moreover, all through Greek literature there runs a ceaseless undercurrent of thought and expression, a note of sadness caused by war's bitterness, its wastefulness, its ruthlessness, the sorrow of the bereft and the pitiless doom of the captive. Ares, the war god, is no glorious figure, even in the *Iliad*, but a savage, repellent being, bane of mortals, for whom the poet bespeaks neither sympathy nor admiration. Themis, Eunomia, Dike, Eirene,—these are the bright goddesses sung alike by Hesiod and by Pindar.[5] Again and again the tragedians, and Aristophanes also, recur to the anxiety and sufferings which war brings in its train, the destruction of property and the sacrifice of life. The Greeks were not a people who delighted in war. Wars there were, —all too frequent, too long, too bitter ; but they were tolerated and not welcomed. To many war seemed an inevitable outcome of human nature or of the organization of society in small city-states ; to others it was an inscrutable ordinance of the divine power, an evil to be shunned as far as might be, but incapable of being wholly eradicated. In answer to those who regarded war as nature's instrument for the reduction of a redundant population, the Greek poets repeatedly pointed out the harmfulness and waste of a method which carried off the strong and brave and left the weakling and the coward to survive.

In such a world as this, where war was a constant and a serious menace, where defeat might entail the subjection or even the destruction of the vanquished community, it is little wonder that the quick intelligence of the Greeks sought for means to avert the outbreak or to mitigate the severity of war. The inscription upon a cenotaph discovered at Corcyra[6] proves that the institution of the προξενία goes back

Sidelights on Greek History

at least to the dawn of the sixth century B.C. The Panhellenic festivals afforded frequent opportunities for friendly intercourse and peaceful rivalry between the citizens of different states, the amphictyonies encouraged at least a partial abandonment of the spirit of jealous exclusiveness. Under the influence of religion and a growing humanitarianism, the full rigours of war were modified, at least in struggles between Greek and Greek. Moral feeling, rather than positive enactment, came to demand a formal declaration of war before the opening of hostilities, the grant of a truce by the victors for the burial of the dead, the liberation of prisoners of war for a recognised ransom. The sacrosanctity of heralds and envoys was normally respected, negotiations became commoner and led to the amicable settlement of many disputes, treaties were concluded and alliances formed—at first for a stipulated number of years and later (not, it would seem, until the early years of the fourth century B.C.) in perpetuity (εἰς τὸν ἅπαντα χρόνον)—and inter-state arbitration was called into being.

Whether the Greeks had been forestalled in this momentous discovery it is impossible to determine with certainty, though there are indications that, in some form, it had not been unknown in the great Oriental Empires long before the emergence of the Greeks into the light of history.[7] But this does not prove that the Greeks were conscious imitators:

they may have been as truly originative in their use of it as if no other power had anticipated them, and to them certainly we owe the development of the institution and its introduction into the Mediterranean world as a recognized and frequent means of settling disputes between state and state and so of averting an appeal to armed force.

The earliest recorded examples of inter-state arbitration in the Greek world belong to the eighth, seventh and sixth centuries B.C., and are preserved solely in the literary evidence, much of which (as, for example, that of Plutarch and Pausanias) is, as we have it, later by many centuries than the events to which it relates. While we may accept at least some of them as historically attested, we must acknowledge the unsatisfactory nature of the sources at our disposal, their lack of detail and the irreconcilable divergences of rival traditions. For the second half of the fifth century we are in a better position, for we have before us the evidence of a competent and contemporary historian, Thucydides. From him we learn that already by 445 B.C. the Greeks had passed beyond the stage at which they had recourse to arbitration only after a dispute had already become acute or had actually led to war. States sometimes pledged themselves in advance to submit to arbitral decision any differences which might arise between them. We have no exact copy of the clause to this effect inserted in the Thirty Years' Peace between Athens and Sparta,[8] but, thanks to the unrevised condition of Books IV. and V. of Thucydides, we know the precise terms of the corresponding clause of the Year's Armistice concluded by these two powers in 423 B.C.,

> 'you shall go to law with us, and we with you, in accordance with ancestral usage, settling our disputes by law without war,' [9]

and again in the Peace of Nicias, two years later,

> 'and if any difference arise between them, let them have recourse to justice and oaths in whatsoever way they may agree.' [10]

And you will remember that, as I pointed out in my last lecture,[11] we have epigraphical proof of the accuracy of Thucydides' copies. "In whatsoever way they may agree": aye, there's the rub. For in the heat of controversy agreement about a method of arbitral settlement is hard, if not impossible, to reach. That is a matter which must be thought out and settled, at least to some extent, in advance, while the blood is still cool and feelings are friendly. And so these clauses failed to avert appeals to arms, which plunged Hellas in disaster and impoverished the world. Yet that fact must not blind us to the significance for human history of the experiment they embody and the aspiration they express. Man climbs but slowly upwards upon the ruins of his hopes and endeavours. And surely it was no small thing that so important a principle had been enunciated, so impressive a warning given to later generations, so striking an appeal made to the human conscience; even Thucydides the realist admits that the Spartans felt uneasy during the Archidamian War because of their rejection of the repeated appeals which Athens had made to the arbitration-clause of the Thirty Years' Peace.[12] Nor did the warning pass wholly unheeded. In later documents we find some attempt made to avoid the fatal indefiniteness which had vitiated the earlier arbitration-clauses. Thus in a treaty between Ephesus and Sardis, mediated by Pergamum, we find the following stipulation:

> 'and if either of the two peoples act in any way contrary to any of the clauses contained in this treaty, the people wronged may receive justice before the state chosen by lot from among those states which they choose in common, the lot being cast by the state which mediates the treaty.' [13]

On the earlier history of Greek inter-state arbitration inscriptions do not, it must be admitted, throw much light. We possess, however, one striking document,—two contiguous fragments of an arbitral award between Cnossus and Tylissus in Crete, issued by, and discovered at, their mother-city Argos,[14]—and this well illustrates some of the salient characteristics of inscriptions. Part of it is wholly lost, part mutilated: it is an isolated scrap, without historical context, without precise date, though probably it falls near the middle of the fifth century: yet, so far as it goes, it gives us information,—contemporary, first-hand, detailed and unquestionably authentic, —of a remarkable attempt to adjust relations and to avoid disputes between two neighbour states.

In the fourth century arbitration seems to have been in fairly common use, but our knowledge is derived mainly from brief references in literature or in the arbitration-records of a later time, which survey the past history of the disputes with which they deal. We have, however, one perfectly preserved award, which, brief as it is, shows the precise and matter-of-fact character of our epigraphical sources. It runs thus :

> ' God. The people of the Argives gave judgement, in accordance with the resolution of the Congress of the Greeks, after the Melians and Cimolians had agreed to abide by whatsoever verdict the Argives should give concerning the islands, that Polyaega, Eterea and Libea belong to the Cimolians. Their verdict was that the Cimolians won their case. Leon was president of the second council, Posidaon secretary of council, Perillus assessor.' [15]

When we pass from the classical to the Hellenistic or the Greco-Roman period, we are aware of a marked change. We learn of a far larger number of cases in which arbitration was employed to settle disputes, alike between states and between individuals, but our knowledge is derived almost wholly from epigraphical records. Literature helps but little. Further, the evidence is drawn from a wide geographical area and concerns many communities which hardly make any appearance in the pages of historical writers. These deal for the most part with the leading states of Hellas and the main currents of Hellenic history, saying little about the minor states and their relations to each other. But the chances of the survival and discovery of an inscription are, as we have already noted, independent of the historical interest of its content.

A further noteworthy change is this, that the relevant inscriptions tend to become much fuller and more prolix than they have previously been, greatly to the detriment of their style when regarded as literary compositions, but equally greatly to the enrichment of our knowledge of the methods of arbitral procedure. Think again of the inscription I have just translated to you. "The people of the Argives gave judgement." How did they do so? Did the Argive citizen assembly hear the evidence and vote upon it? or was it represented by a tribunal? if so, was that tribunal large or small? were its members appointed by lot or selected as possessing special qualifications? what kind of evidence was brought before it? was its verdict unanimous or that of a majority? To these and other questions which present themselves the inscription affords no reply. It tells only of the invitation addressed to Argos by the Congress of the Greeks, the consent of the disputants, the award of the arbitrators and the date of

Sidelights on Greek History 49

its issue. Many of the later epigraphical documents, on the other hand, contain detailed accounts of the size, composition and appointment of the tribunal, its procedure, the evidence adduced by both parties, the considerations which led the arbitrators to their verdict and the full text of the award itself. Thus they give us not mere glimpses but minute descriptions of the machinery and processes of arbitration, a subject upon which literature hardly ever has a word to spare.

By way of illustration, let me put side by side the literary and the epigraphical account of the one case of arbitration for which we possess evidence of both kinds.

Tacitus' history of the year A.D. 25 contains a statement[16] that Lacedaemonian and Messenian embassies came to Rome to plead before the Senate the claims of their states to the border territory known as the ager Dentheliates and to the temple of Artemis Limnatis which lay within it. The Messenians declared that Philip of Macedon, Antigonus and Mummius had decided the dispute in their favour, and added that the Milesians had pronounced in the same sense when officially asked to arbitrate (*sic Milesios permisso publice arbitrio decrevisse*), as had also, in the last instance, Atidius Geminus, the governor of Achaea.

" The Milesians had decided in the same sense " : that is all Tacitus tells us. Turn now to an inscription[17] discovered at Olympia engraved on the base of Paeonius' famous statue of Victory. It bears the title

> 'Award in territorial dispute between Messenians and Lacedaemonians,'

and comprises three documents, almost completely preserved. The first is an Elean decree, recording the visit of three Messenian envoys bearing an assurance of good will and a request for permission to engrave at Olympia the Milesian award relative to the territory claimed by Messenia and Sparta, reciprocating that assurance, granting that request and honouring those envoys. Next follows the full text of a letter from the Milesian magistrates to those of the Eleans, accompanying a copy of the award in question, authenticated by the public seal of Miletus. And lastly we have the award itself, which opens with a precise indication of the date and then proceeds thus:

> 'A plenary assembly was convened in the theatre on the aforesaid day, as was agreed by the Lacedaemonians and Messenians, and 600 judges were appointed by lot from the whole people, the largest tribunal allowed by the laws, and the case was introduced in accordance with the letter of the aforesaid praetor and with the decree of the Senate relative to the dispute of the Lacedaemonians and Messenians, on the understanding that whoever of them possessed this territory when Lucius Mummius was in that province as consul or proconsul should continue so to possess it. And the

water was divided between them in order to measure their speeches, fifteen Milesian *metretae* for the first speech on either side and five Milesian *metretae* for the second speech, as they themselves also approved. And after Eudamidas son of Euthycles had spoken on the Lacedaemonian side and Nicis the son of Nicon on the Messenian side with due observance of the water, and when the speeches had been spoken by them both, it was decided that the territory had been in the possession of the Messenians when Lucius Mummius was in that province as consul or proconsul, and that these should continue so to possess it. Of the votes, 584 were given for the view that the territory had been in the possession of the Messenians and that these should continue so to possess it, 16 for the view that it had been in the possession of the Lacedaemonians.'

How precise, how detailed is the picture here presented! how marked the contrast between it and Tacitus' bald outline! I am not, let me say emphatically, criticizing Tacitus. He has selected that which was germane to his purpose and has expressed it correctly and tersely. Even had he known, which almost certainly he did not, the *dossier* engraved at Olympia, he could not have inserted in his *Annals* a translation of it without laying himself open to a charge of disproportion or even irrelevance. The nature of the verdict alone concerned him, the manner in which it was reached was of secondary interest. But for us, who seek to understand not only the occasions but also the processes of ancient arbitration, inscriptions such as this are of inestimable value.

Nor does the document which I have just brought before you represent by any means the highest degree of elaboration and detail which such records reach. An arbitral tribunal sometimes sought to justify, alike to contemporaries and to posterity, the verdict which it passed by the publication of a more or less lengthy report (ἔκθεσις). This might contain not merely the date of the trial, the terms of reference, an account of the appointment, personnel and procedure of the tribunal and the full text of the award, but also a *précis*, or even on occasion a verbal quotation, of the evidence which had been adduced by either side and a reasoned exposition of the considerations which had led the court to its decision. Of especial interest from this point of view is the long record of an arbitration undertaken, on the invitation of the Roman Senate, by the people of Magnesia on the Maeander in a territorial dispute between two important cities of eastern Crete, Itanus and Hierapytna.[18] The story is a lengthy and a complicated one and I cannot enter into it here. Dr. Cary has rendered a valuable service in unravelling the tangled skein, and to his article in the *Journal of Roman Studies*[19] I refer you, though I cannot refrain from quoting from it two sentences. " It is clear that the second Magnesian jury performed its task in a

Sidelights on Greek History

thoroughly businesslike way. Its report, it is true, is long-winded and ill-arranged; but its findings are amply supported by documentary and circumstantial proofs, and they reveal a very sound sense of judicial evidence." With this judgement I am in complete agreement. Nor does this case appear to me to constitute an exception to the general rule. Eighteen years ago I closed my chapter on the evidence adduced in arbitral trials with these words: " The impression we receive from a careful review of the extant records is favourable alike to the thoroughness with which the courts examined all the available evidence and to the conscientiousness with which they arrived at their final verdict."[20] The fresh evidence which has accumulated in the intervening years has served to strengthen rather than to weaken that impression.

So vital is this aspect of our study to a proper appreciation of the methods and the value of Greek arbitration that I need not apologize for calling your attention to two further documents, which well illustrate the character and variety of the arguments employed to gain a favourable decision. Both of them relate to disputes between Samos and Priene.

On a stone found at Samos, and now preserved in the Ashmolean Museum at Oxford, is engraved a rescript[21] addressed to the Samians by King Lysimachus of Thrace towards the close of his reign, i.e., shortly before 281 B.C. In this he informs them of the course and result of the arbitration he has undertaken between the Samians and their neighbours on the mainland, and at the outset almost apologetically explains a misunderstanding which led him to promise his intervention as arbitrator. Let me translate in full this first paragraph.

> 'King Lysimachus to the council and people of the Samians, greeting. The envoys sent from you and those sent from the Prienians with reference to the territory to which they had previously raised a claim in our presence, appeared before us. Now had we known beforehand that you possessed and cultivated this territory for so many years past, we should not at all have undertaken the decision : but, as it was, we were under the impression that your entry upon it happened quite a short time ago, for so the envoys of the Prienians in their former speeches spoke of it to us. However, since the envoys from you and also those from the Prienians were here, we could not but give a hearing to the statements made on both sides.'

Then follows the king's summary of the arguments used by the Prienians. Their original claim to the disputed territory they sought to establish by an appeal to " the histories and the other testimonies and claims, together with the six years' truce." Later, they admitted, in face of the inroad into Ionia made by a horde of invaders (in whom we may recognize the Cimmerians of Herodotus i. 15) under the leadership of Lygdamis, the territory had been evacuated by all its Greek occupants and the Samians had retired to their island. The withdrawal of Lygdamis had been followed by the return of the Prienians to their possessions, but not a single Samian had taken part in this resettlement with the exception of a few who were residents (κάτοικοι) at Priene, and these paid to the Prienians the taxes due from them. Later, the Samians came back and forcibly seized and held the territory until a settlement was effected by the Prienian envoy Bias, the famous sage of that name. Thus down to quite recent times the territory had been in Prienian possession, and in consequence they asked for its restoration to them as its original owners.

Then comes a summary of the counter-pleas adduced by the Samian representatives, of which unfortunately only the first few clauses survive on the stone. It was followed, we may safely assume, by the summing up of King Lysimachus and the formulation of his award. That this was in favour of the Samians we may judge alike from the fact that this record was erected at Samos[22] and from the tone of the opening sentences of the rescript, which I have already translated.

It is not necessary for my present purpose to enter into a detailed examination of the long and chequered history of the dispute which eventually called for Lysimachus' intervention as arbitrator. Those who wish to do so will find invaluable help in an article[23] by Professor U. von Wilamowitz-Moellendorff, which contains the best available reading and restoration of the greater part of the document in question. To two points, however, I wish briefly to call your attention before I pass on. Note, first, the time and trouble devoted to the settlement of this difference by the ruler of a wide empire, the fair and dispassionate tone which characterizes his rescript, and his evident desire to justify his award to the reason and the conscience of the states directly concerned and of the world at large. And, in the second place, note that, so far as our knowledge goes, this arbitration of Lysimachus closed for ever a dispute which had lasted, in varying degrees of intensity, for four centuries at least.

Even fuller and more interesting is the next document to which I turn,[24] engraved on a number of blocks which originally formed part of the south *anta* and the south *cella*-wall of the temple of Athena at Priene and are now housed in the British Museum. Once again the disputants are the Samians and the Prienians, but the question at issue, though a territorial one, is not that of Batinetus and the surrounding land, which Lysimachus had settled a century earlier. This time it is no powerful monarch who arbitrates, nor yet a large popular tribunal, embodying the democratic ideal of justice, like that court of six hundred Milesians who, as we have seen, adjudicated on the Spartan and Messenian claims to the ager Dentheliates. The matter is referred to the

Rhodian state and from its members a panel of five arbitrators is selected, a small body of men chosen, we may assume, for their character and ability. At the close of their proceedings they drew up a report upon the whole case and this reflects credit upon the clarity of their thought and expression, the thoroughness with which they carried out the task entrusted to them and the equitable nature of their final judgement, which was, as we learn from another inscription, confirmed by a *senatus consultum* about half a century later, by a second *senatus consultum* dated 136 B.C. and by a further arbitral award.[25]

Time does not permit me to offer you a translation, or even a full summary, of this report, which forms a document more than 170 lines long, excluding certain fragments whose attribution to it appears questionable ; but I cannot pass on without a brief indication of its structure and a few remarks on some of its salient features. After the title, which records the two parties to the arbitration, follow the names of the five citizens elected by the Rhodian people, at the request of the Samians and the Prienians, to form a tribunal which is to

> 'judge the case and determine the frontier and issue an award or bring about an agreed settlement,' [26]

and a reference to the controversy, which concerned certain disputed territory and a fort named Carium.

In passing let me say that it is characteristic of

the practice of Greek arbitrators to seek, if possible, to arrive at an equitable solution which might be voluntarily accepted by both sides, and so to end the quarrel by mediation rather than by arbitration proper.[27] Thus one arbitral court draws attention to the fact that it postponed the issue of its award " in order that sufficient time should be allowed to the disputants to arrive at an agreed settlement," while in another case it is laid down that the arbitrators shall give their verdict on oath

> ' and their decisions ($κριθέντα$) shall be binding and unalterable ; likewise they shall inscribe upon a stele the agreements arrived at ($συνλυθέντα$), if accepted by both parties.'[28]

The motive which prompted this procedure is not far to seek. Mediation was a more friendly method of settlement than the exercise of the judicial authority vested in arbitrators. It gave to the victorious party all that it could equitably claim, but spared to some extent the susceptibilities of the vanquished. Moreover, it was felt that this method was more likely to foster a friendly feeling and to " pave the way for a better understanding between the states involved and thus render the recurrence of similar differences in the future less probable." This constantly reiterated anxiety to settle quarrels upon the basis best calculated to lead to " the restoration of the original friendship " between the disputants does credit alike to the heads and to the hearts of the arbitrators, and

Sidelights on Greek History 59

we can enter even now into the disappointment with which the members of a Magnesian court record the failure of their efforts at conciliation :

> 'but when our purpose failed of its fulfilment owing to the excessive embitterment which had sprung up between them, it befell that the verdict was decided by the vote.'[29]

But we must now turn back to the Rhodian report. After giving the names of the representatives selected by each state to advocate its claims (five by the Prienians and an uncertain number by the Samians), it proceeds, in a paragraph which I translate as affording an illustration of the pains taken by the ancient arbitrators to find a firm ground for their awards, thus :

> 'And after we had given them a full hearing, alike at Rhodes in the temple of Dionysus and on the territory in dispute, to which each of the two parties conducted us, and at the fort which bears the name of Carium and at Ephesus in the temple of Artemis, we arrived at our decision in accordance with what we had seen.'[30]

Then comes the verdict, short and clear, awarding the fort and the surrounding territory to the Prienians, followed by a recital of the names of the Samian and the Prienian magistrates to whom a copy of the verdict was handed and the exact date on which they received it.

But this admirably arranged survey of the *acta* of

the Rhodian tribunal[31] occupies only one seventh, or even less, of the whole document. To it are appended long and careful summaries of the evidence brought forward by the Samians in three speeches and by the Prienians in two, followed by a statement,[32] in which the judges summarize the evidence as a whole, trace chronologically the history of the dispute and conclude with a reasoned justification of their award. It would be interesting to possess this section in its entirety, but unfortunately seven or eight of the forty-eight or forty-nine lines which it originally comprised have wholly perished, while of twenty-four others half, or less than half, survives, so that a satisfactory restoration is unattainable. Nevertheless, enough is left to give us an impression of the difficulty and complexity of the task which confronted the arbitrators and of the conscientious thoroughness with which they addressed themselves to it. The opening lines of this section are especially worthy of notice, for they suggest the historical research and even the literary criticism which the tribunal must needs undertake.

> 'Now we, bearing in view the fact that, of those who wrote the story of the Meliac War and the partition of the territory, all the rest stated that as a result of the partition the Samians received as their portion Phygela, although four of them were Samians, viz., Uliades and Olympichus and Duris and Euagon, and two Ephesians, viz., Creophylus and Eualces, and one a Chian, Theopompus, all of

whom we find have left it on record that they received as their portion Phygela, and only in the histories which bear the name of Maeandrius of Miletus is it put on record that the Samians received as their portion Carium and Dryussa,—histories which many of the authors challenge, maintaining that they bear a false title, . . .' [33]

Here the text breaks off, and we are left breathless and wondering how many more words besides the seventy-nine which are extant separate the " we," with which the sentence opens, from the verb of which it is the subject. But though the expression may be ponderous, the thought is clear and easy to follow, and we may well imagine the bitterness of the Samian advocates, when they found their carefully prepared arguments refuted by the evidence of four Samian historians among others.

But a further task awaited the Rhodian arbitrators after the evidence had been investigated, the award pronounced and written copies of it officially delivered to the authorities of the two states concerned. The disputed frontier must be carefully and clearly demarcated, and so we find at the close of the document a detailed description of the frontier and of the positions of the engraved boundary-marks left by the Rhodians.[34] Nor is this by any means a unique example of a frontier-delimitation preserved in a Greek inscription. Three documents containing such delimitations were offered as evidence by the Itanians in their dispute with their Hierapytnian neighbours and were admitted by the latter as genuine, and in the Magnesian report on the case their crucial passages are quoted *verbatim*. Or we may call to mind the brief, but perfectly preserved, record of a boundary award in a dispute between Oeniadae and Metropolis :

> 'Territorial decision of the district of Stratus. The following is the decision of the land-judges (γαο-δίκαι) of the Thyrrheans. Boundaries of the land between Oeniadae and the Metropolitans : the dividing wall and from the dividing wall in a straight line through the marsh to the sea. And let the city of Oeniadae and the city of Metropolis inscribe the decision at Thermum in the temple of Apollo.' [35]

Another well known example,[36] dating from about 240 B.C., is that of a territorial dispute between Corinth and Epidaurus, settled in favour of the latter by a tribunal of 151 Megarians : the Corinthians raised difficulties about the precise position of the boundary line and, as it was obviously impracticable for so large a body as 151 to survey and delimit the frontier, thirty-one of them were chosen for this purpose and fixed the frontier in a manner described in full detail in the surviving record.

I am aware that I have not given you in this lecture any systematic account of the history and working of inter-state arbitration in the Greek world. Such has not been my object. I essayed that task in the little work to which I have already referred, and, although in the light of further discoveries I should like to introduce into it a few modifications and many additions, I believe that in the main the picture there drawn remains true to the facts as we now know them. My aim this evening has rather been to illustrate the peculiar nature and value of the contribution made by inscriptions to our knowledge of this aspect of the public life of the Greek states, not only by adding to our list of arbitral settlements a large number of cases wholly unknown to our literary records, but by enabling us to examine in detail the working of the institution. It is to them that we must turn if we wish to learn what classes of disputes, whether actual or contingent, were submitted to arbitration, what individuals, councils or states were chosen as arbitrators, upon what conditions they undertook their tasks and by what methods they fulfilled them, upon what kinds of evidence their awards were based, how those awards were determined, formulated, communicated to the disputant states and published to the world at large, and what penalties were attached to any infraction of them.

But there remains one general question to which you will expect me to furnish some kind of reply: was arbitration a success in the ancient Greek world?[37] Before we can return any answer, we must define more closely what we mean by two of the terms here employed. What do we mean by "arbitration"? its bare existence, or its actual use?

There is a profound difference between these two. The mere existence of a medicine will work no cures, its application may heal, or at least alleviate, disease. So also in the case of arbitration. Its recognition as a possibility, an aspiration, a promise, an ideal will neither avert nor terminate a dispute; it does not work automatically, but must be brought into operation. And its failure is no more demonstrated by a reference to the constant wars from which the Greek world suffered than the ineffectiveness of a medicine is proved by the continued ill-health of one who refuses or neglects to take it.

But again, what do we mean by " success " ? Is the police force a " success " ? It exists largely for the purpose of preventing—and, if this primary object is not attained, of punishing—crime. Yet crimes are committed daily and some of the perpetrators escape detection and penalty. Is medical science a " success " ? Its aim is to alleviate and to cure the ailments to which the bodies and minds of men are subject. But disease is still with us, and some forms of it continue to baffle every effort of medical research to discover a remedy. Was arbitration a " success " ? If what we are really asking is whether the existence and recognition of the arbitral method and its prescription in the form of arbitration-clauses in many treaties effectually eradicated war among the Greek states, our answer will, of course, be a decided negative. War was rampant in the Greek world throughout its history, although it tends to be unduly emphasized in our ancient records and the peaceful community is like to have no history. Appeals to the arbitral settlement of disputes were sometimes rejected. Disputes in which an arbitral decision had been given were often subsequently re-opened and required fresh settlement. All this is undeniable; yet who that studies attentively these ancient records will dare to speak of arbitration as a failure? How small a proportion of the cases known to us as settled by an arbitral award were later re-opened! And when this happens, the appeal is never to arms but always to a fresh arbitration. In our discussion of this subject we must bear constantly in mind the alternative to arbitration. It was not negotiation, for the very appeal to an arbiter presupposes the failure of negotiation, but war, with all its attendant evils and with no guarantee either of justice or of finality in its verdict. Our records, especially our epigraphical records, tell us of a large number of cases in which arbitration was tried. In the majority of these it seems, so far as our knowledge goes, to have worked an immediate and lasting cure; in a small minority, a temporary alleviation only. The disease here was perhaps incurable; incurable it certainly appeared so far as the expedients known to that age were concerned, and it was no slight benefit that arbitration could at least keep it in check by being administered from time to time as occasion demanded. But the documents I have brought before your notice, and those many others of which they are typical, will, I hope, show that arbitration did serve a valuable purpose in averting wars or in bringing to a speedier end conflicts which had already broken out, as well as in accustoming men to look for the settlement of their disputes not to force but to reason and equity.

NOTES ON LECTURE II

[1] *De arbitrio inter liberas Graecorum civitates*, Paris.

[2] *L'arbitrage international chez les Hellènes*, Christiania.

[3] *International Arbitration amongst the Greeks*, Oxford.

[4] Cf. W. E. Caldwell, *Hellenic Conceptions of Peace*, New York, 1919 : to this work I owe several of the references used in this and the following paragraph.

[5] Hesiod, *Theog.* 901–3, Pindar, *Ol.* xiii. 6–8.

[6] *I.G.* ix. 1. 867.

[7] Tod, *op. cit.* 170 ff.

[8] Thuc. i. 78.4, 140.2, 144.2, 145, vii. 18.2.

[9] Thuc. iv. 118. 8.

[10] Thuc. v. 18. 4.

[11] See p. 26.

[12] Thuc. vii. 18. 2.

[13] *O.G.I.* 437. 73 ff.

[14] *S.I.G.* 56.

[15] *S.I.G.* 261, Hicks and Hill, *Greek Hist. Inscr.* 150.

[16] *Annals*, iv. 43.

[17] *S.I.G.* 683.

[18] *S.I.G.* 685 ; cf. *S.E.G.* ii. 511.

[19] xvi. 194 ff.

[20] Tod, *op. cit.* 151.

[21] *O.G.I.* 13, *Inschriften von Priene*, 500.

[22] Tod, *op. cit.* 157.
[23] *Sitzungsberichte der Berl. Akad.* 1906, 39 ff.
[24] *Inschriften von Priene*, 37, 38.
[25] *Ibid.* 40, 41, 42.
[26] L. 12 f.
[27] Cf. Tod., *op cit.* 123 ff.
[28] *O.G.I.* 335. 31 ff.
[29] *S.I.G.* 685. 35 ff.
[30] L. 20 ff.
[31] Ll. 1—44.
[32] L. 118 ff.
[33] Ll. 118—123.
[34] L. 158 ff.
[35] *S.I.G.* 421. 44 ff.
[36] *S.I.G.* 471.
[37] Cf. Tod, *op. cit.* 184 ff.

LECTURE III

CLUB AND SOCIETIES IN THE GREEK WORLD

LECTURE III

Clubs and Societies in the Greek World

IN the two preceding lectures I have drawn your attention to some of the salient characteristics of Greek inscriptions regarded as evidence for the life and thought of the ancient Greeks, and have illustrated those characteristics by special reference to the topic of inter-state arbitration in the Greek world. In the present lecture I deal with a topic taken from the private life of the Greeks, that of the organization and activities of the Greek clubs and societies.

And, first, let us briefly survey the evidence at our disposal for the purpose of this study. This is almost wholly epigraphical, for the papyri, though by no means negligible, relate solely to Ptolemaic and Roman Egypt,[1] while literature maintains an almost unbroken silence on the subject, a silence all the more remarkable when we bear in mind the widespread diffusion, the long history and the unquestionable popularity of the Greek clubs. Fortunately, the number of relevant inscriptions is very large[2] and we are embarrassed rather by the abundance than by the meagreness of our materials. They are drawn from a wide area, practically coextensive with the Greek world, and thus reflect for us the usages not of a single state or locality but of the Greek people as a whole. They also cover a long period, from the fourth century B.C. down to the third century of the Christian era : indeed, there was probably no break between the associations they commemorate and the Byzantine guilds known to us chiefly from the edict of Leo the Wise which is commonly called the ἐπαρχικὸν βιβλίον.³ P. Foucart collected and discussed the evidence for religious associations among the Greeks in an important work⁴ published in 1873, but this has been to a large extent superseded by the more recent and more comprehensive studies of E. Ziebarth⁵ and F. Poland,⁶ which appeared in 1896 and 1909 respectively. So far as I am aware, no discussion of the subject as a whole exists in our own language, and no brief, readable and up-to-date account in any language.⁷

That there were voluntary associations in the Greek world from an early time is antecedently probable and is confirmed by a law of Solon, the text of which was quoted by Gaius in his commentary on the Twelve Tables.⁸ This law did not create corporations, but it recognized their legality and made their regulations binding upon their members provided that they were not contrary to the laws of the state. Again, there is a famous passage in Thucydides,⁹ relative to the movement of στάσις which swept over the Greek states during the Peloponnesian War like some virulent plague, in which there are references to the ἑταιρίαι, or political associations, as playing a prominent part, while elsewhere[10] the historian speaks of the activities of such secret societies, there called ξυνωμοσίαι ἐπὶ δίκαις καὶ ἀρχαῖς, in augurating a reign of terror and paving the way for the subversion of the Athenian democracy in 411. But these notices are almost isolated, and it is not until we reach the Hellenistic age that we can trace the remarkably rapid development of club life over the whole Greek world which is attested by scores, or rather by hundreds, of inscriptions. Nor is the reason of this, I venture to think, far to seek. In the classical period the life of the citizen was closely and almost exclusively bound up with that of the state: the πολίτης was a member of his πόλις, and he was little or nothing besides. "Man," Aristotle declared,[11] "is by nature a political animal." His social instincts were fully satisfied by the family, the phratry, the deme, the tribe, to which he belonged, as well as by the state itself; each of these had its own meetings, its festivals, its varied opportunities of enjoyment and good-fellowship. His religious aspirations were met, to a large extent though not wholly, by the worships connected with these bodies. And this satisfaction of social and religious cravings and ambitions left little or no room for the formation of voluntary societies. But in course of time the old simplicity gave way to a greater complexity of life. An increasing cosmopolitanism took the place of the old exclusiveness, while the growth of the empires of Macedon and of the successors of Alexander robbed Greece of her autonomy and sounded the death-knell of much that was characteristic of the old city-state. Men lost their political ideals and their civic enthusiasm and turned more deliberately to the pursuit of wealth or of pleasure.

But it was above all the desire for religious fellowship and common worship that contributed to the formation of guilds within the state. New cults spread rapidly and were but slowly, if at all, taken up into the established religion. The earliest societies of which we have epigraphical records, those of the ὀργεῶνες,[12] are essentially religious in character, existing for the cult of some deity or hero and at first confined to citizens. Such a body of ὀργεῶνες met in the fourth century in a little chapel on the western slope of the Acropolis for the cult of the hero Amynus, with whom were associated Asclepius and the poet Sophocles, worshipped as the hero Dexion, and other similar societies, the ὀργεῶνες of the Mother of the gods and those of Bendis, are also attested by fourth-century inscriptions. Then come the societies of θιασῶται,[13] some of which can be traced back to the same century, still primarily religious, but with a far more developed social side; these consisted largely of aliens rather than of citizens and sometimes formed national clubs, the members of which were compatriots in a foreign land united primarily for the worship of their national divinities. In course of time, however, the religious aim tends to fall into the background. The scope of the gild is widened, its resources grow, its organization is developed ; more and more the social and economic basis takes the place of the religious. Characteristic of this stage are the societies of ἐρανισταί,[14] which flourished from the middle of the third century B.C. down to Imperial times. In them the religious element is not wholly absent ; they perform certain religious acts and frequently bear in their titles the names of gods : but in essence they are social and economic, and worship is of subordinate interest. Finally, we find, both in Athens and elsewhere, a number of purely secular σύνοδοι.[15]

Time will not allow me to dwell at any length upon the terminology[16] of these clubs or societies : but a few words must be said in passing. The general titles, to which I have referred, may be replaced by others, which are of a more specific nature. Thus various societies of θιασῶται are called συνθύται, μύσται, ἱερουργοί, μελανηφόροι, μολποί and so on, while the ἐρανισταί bear such titles as συμβιωταί, συνήθεις, φίλοι, ἀδελφοί and others ; in the former group you will notice the religious, in the latter the social, implication of the terms used. In the names of individual associations three types predominate. (1) Most common are the names derived from the gods in whose honour the societies were established and whose cults formed the centres of their respective worships; e.g., Ἀπολλωνιασταί, Διονυσιασταί, Ἡρακλεῖσταί. Sometimes a single society unites several cults, as the Rhodian κοινὸν Σωτηριαστᾶν Διοσξενιαστᾶν Παναθαναϊστᾶν Λινδιαστᾶν. We know of about a hundred associations whose names are of this type. (2) Other societies derive their names from their founders, reformers, or presidents, as the κοινὸν τὸ Νικομάχειον at Chalcedon. (3) In other titles the name of some locality or nationality is prominent. This may refer either to the nationality of the members or to the place at which the club is established. Examples of the former type abound, especially in the great trading centres of Athens, Piraeus, Delos and Rhodes, where foreign merchants and seamen gathered in large numbers. Thus at Piraeus we find a club of Αἰγύπτιοι, another of Κιτιεῖς or οἱ ἔμποροι τῶν Κιτιέων, a third of Cyprian Σαλαμίνιοι, and one of Σιδώνιοι. Examples of the second type of geographical name are οἱ ἐν Δήλῳ τραπεζῖται, οἱ ἐν Ἐφέσῳ ἐργάται προπυλεῖται. These three types of names may be illustrated by those of three great London Hospitals, St. Bartholomew's, Guy's, Charing Cross, where also we see the use of religious, human and local terms.

Of the epithets[17] attached to societies the commonest is ἱερός or ἱερώτατος, which is not only applied to religious and mystic associations and becomes a standing epithet of the agonistic guilds, but is also freely used by trade-guilds, as the ἱερὰ φυλὴ τῶν ἐριουργῶν at Philadelphia, the ἱερώτατον συνέδριον τῶν ἁλιέων at Cyzicus and the ἱερώτατον συνέδριον τῶν σακκοφόρων λιμενειτῶν, "the most sacred association of porter dockers," at Panormus. The title σεβαστός—"worshipful," the regular epithet of our City Companies,—is rare, but φιλοσέβαστος, "loyal," is common. Other epithets used are μέγας, οἰκουμενικός, σεμνότατος and a group of terms used to distinguish two similar guilds in the same town, e.g., παλαιός, νέος, πρῶτοι, πρεσβύτεροι, γνήσιοι. The use of αὐτόνομοι, "independent," recalls a common epithet of friendly societies and similar bodies, e.g., the Independent Order of Rechabites.

We may now turn to the societies themselves and their activities. I shall make no attempt to classify them, for a satisfactory classification is well-nigh impossible, and that for several reasons. The first is the bewildering variety of their nature and their aims. Again, the aim of a society may be composite and vague instead of single and well defined. It may blend religious worship and social intercourse, commercial advantage and education. Aristotle's dictum,[18] that societies exist either for the sake of gain or for that of pleasure, does not help us much; for these two ends are not sharply distinguishable, and many of the societies known to us seem to have sought after both simultaneously. Further, it is often difficult or impossible for us to infer the nature of a society from its title, and of many of the Greek guilds nothing at all is known except their names. Modern illustrations are not hard to find. What would you conclude about the purposes and activities of those great societies in our midst—Freemasons, Druids, Free Foresters, Oddfellows, Buffaloes and the like—if you knew nothing about them save their titles?

It will, I think, serve our purpose best if, out of the great variety of clubs and associations which meet us in the ancient records, I select a single group by way of illustration and say something about the trade-guilds of the Greek world.[19]

In early times, certain callings, especially those demanding a high degree of science or skill, tended to be hereditary. The father taught his sons the secrets of his craft ; the knowledge was confined within the family and thus its full value was secured. We can trace in ancient times through several generations families of sculptors and of doctors. Indeed, it is in the medical profession that we can see most clearly the transition from the family to the guild. We know little, it is true, except about the famous medical school of Cos ; of that, however, we learn much from the writings of Hippocrates and Galen. Originally the medical science and art passed from father to son, but as early as the time of Hippocrates the transition had begun. For, according to Plato,[20] Hippocrates accepted payment for medical tuition. In other words, the apprentice-system had begun; a stranger could be received into the school on taking an oath, the exact formula of which is preserved, and membership of the body was shared by all ὡρκισμένοι μαθηταί. Thus the family expands into a brotherhood and the foundations are laid of the future development of the Greek and Byzantine trade-guild and of its medieval counterpart.

In what trades and industries do we find traces of this organization? It is most common among those engaged in the production of clothing, whether of wool or of linen. Thus we find guilds of wool-workers (ἐριουργοί), weavers, wool-washers (ἐριοπλύται), wool-merchants (λανάριοι), dyers (βαφεῖς), purple-dyers (πορφυροβάφοι) and fullers (γναφεῖς). Less frequent are the guilds of linen-workers (λινουργοί), linen-weavers (λινύφοι) and linen-sellers (λινοπῶλαι); only once, at Thyatira, do we meet with a clothiers' union (ἱματευόμενοι), and even its existence has recently been questioned.[21] Industries dealing with leather are also well represented. Tanners (βυρσεῖς, σκυτοβυρσεῖς) and cobblers have their unions in various towns of Asia Minor, at Mytilene and in Egypt and in their titles make a special claim to be regarded as artists (τεχνῖται).

The metal industry likewise affords a wide field for such associations, and I would ask you to notice in passing the high pitch to which the division of labour is carried. Goldsmiths and silversmiths, workers in bronze and in iron, solderers (χαλκοκολληταί), knife-makers (μαχαιροποιοί), bedstead-manufacturers (κλινοπηγοί), nail-makers (ἡλοκόποι) and metal-polishers are found in inscriptions forming their several guilds, especially in Asia Minor and in Egypt. Stone-workers of various kinds are similarly organized,—stone-workers (λιθουργοί), sculptors (λατύποι), stone-masons (λατόμοι), stone-polishers (λιθοξόοι), marble-cutters (μαρμαράριοι) and even, it would seem, carvers of coral ornaments (κοραλλιοπλάσται). So also are builders and carpenters.

Industries connected with the food-supply are less represented, though we find, especially in Egypt, guilds of farmers, gardeners, bee-keepers, greengrocers, oil-vendors, beer-dealers, bakers, millers and fishermen.

Perinthus has its barbers' guild and Egypt a number of societies composed of those engaged in the various processes of embalming and burying (ταριχευταί, νεκροτάφοι, etc.). Finally, we have glimpses of the same kind of organization among transport-workers: at Smyrna there were at least two guilds of porters (φορτηγοί) and alike at Perinthus and at Cyzicus we find societies of sack-carriers (σακκοφόροι).

No less remarkable was the principle of association among the great merchants, especially those visiting, or resident in, foreign ports, than among the artisan and labouring classes. At Athens we find clubs of wholesale merchants (ἔμποροι) and shippers (ναύκληροι), while at Delos a third body, the warehousemen (ἐγδοχεῖς), are associated with them: the two wealthiest and most prominent of the Delian corporations were those composed of merchants, shippers and warehousemen from Tyre and from Beyrout, the former united for the cult of Heracles, the latter for that of Poseidon. The remains of the large and splendidly equipped club-house of the latter society have been laid bare by the spade and carefully studied.[22] Similar associations no doubt existed also at Rhodes, a great cosmopolitan trade-centre in which there was a remarkably vigorous development of club-life.

You will notice that so far I have carefully avoided the use of the term trade-union in speaking of these guilds. Of their activities we are ill-informed and we must be on our guard against over-emphasizing the similarity between them and the modern trade-union. In the first place, these ancient societies were almost entirely local; at most they extended over an island or an Egyptian province. We hear, for example, of οἱ κατὰ τὴν νῆσον ἀρχιτέκτονες in Cyprus and of the bakers' guild of the Arsinoite νομός, but it is highly improbable that the οἰκουμενικὸν καὶ σεμνότατον συνέδριον τῶν λινουργῶν at Miletus was even provincial, still less was it worldwide. The modern trade-union, on the other hand, is national or even, to some extent, international.

Again, the trade-guilds of antiquity were primarily, or even exclusively, religious and social, and did not normally seek to regulate or modify the conditions under which industry was carried on. And this is true also of the merchants' guilds at Delos and elsewhere. It is improbable that they engaged corporately in commercial undertakings or attempted to restrict the freedom of their members in business enterprises. The part played by these associations approximated, let us say, to that played by the British Club and the English Church in some foreign commercial centre, such as Bordeaux or Rotterdam.

And, thirdly, the associations which we are considering do not represent the combination of labour in its struggle with capital. They are not bodies of employees as distinct from, or even opposed to, employers. Most of their members were probably at work on their own account, others were employers of small bodies of slaves or free labourers, others again were so employed; but if we call them trade-unions, we must remember that they are simultaneously masters' federations. And one of the reasons, it appears to me, why the industrial history of the ancient world is, so far as we know it, so free from the convulsions and struggles which mark its political history is that these societies afforded constant opportunities to those engaged, in whatsoever capacity, in the same industry, trade or profession to meet together for common worship and social intercourse, and thus to foster a spirit of brotherhood and sympathy.

Not that labour troubles were wholly absent from the ancient world, but they do not seem to take the form of struggles between masters and men. In a recent essay[23] Mr. W. H. Buckler has edited and discussed four epigraphical records of labour disputes in the Roman province of Asia. One of these, assigned by its first editors to Magnesia on the Maeander but now rightly claimed for Ephesus,[24] contains a rescript of the Roman governor relative to a strike which the bakers' union had threatened or perhaps even begun. The bakers are ordered to continue their work on pain of severe penalties and for the future all meetings of the union are forbidden.

Within the narrow limits of this lecture I cannot attempt to summarize the rich store of information about the organization, cults, finances and officials of the Greek societies afforded by extant inscriptions. One or two matters, however, demand a passing mention.

Some societies comprised a limited number of members; others had no such restriction. Speaking generally, few seem to have contained less than ten members, few to have surpassed a hundred, and the average may be reckoned at about thirty to thirty-five.[25]

In character this membership was very varied. Women sometimes formed clubs of their own, sometimes they are found side by side with men : one Attic ἔρανος, for example, contained thirty-seven men and twenty-one women, while the membership of another was composed of fifty-nine men and thirty-four women. Outside Attica—and this fact calls for special notice—women play a much smaller part in the extant club-records, and, were it not for the family-associations, which included women, and the need for priestesses in certain cults, we might say that the development of club-life affected women but little outside of Attica. Children, too, were sometimes admitted ; thus the Athenian Iobacchi and the Pergamene ὑμνῳδοί accepted at reduced rates the children of members so long as they were under age and admitted them to the guild-festivals, though allowing them only a half-portion of food and wine. Slaves and freedmen sometimes formed societies of their own,—e.g., that of the Diosatabyriastae at Rhodes and the ἔρανος founded at Sunium for slaves and by a slave in the first or second century of our era, the remarkable regulations of which have survived.[26] In other clubs slaves and free men are fellow-members, and it was surely a matter of no small moment that these guilds united in a common religious and social life elements of society otherwise rigidly sundered and so contributed to bridge a gulf seemingly impassable. Further, the clubs promoted friendly intercourse between citizens and aliens, especially in the cosmopolitan centres such as Piraeus, Delos and Rhodes. In Attica societies composed exclusively of foreigners seem always to have been in a minority, and the readiness of Athenians to join associations in which foreigners preponderated is a striking phenomenon. The Rhodian clubs, too, and still more those of Delos, show a large proportion of aliens in their membership.

Admission to a club was gained by the vote of the existing members. The candidate made his application, his case was considered and a vote was taken. If this proved favourable, he had to pay an entrance-fee and, in some cases at least, swear to observe the society's regulations. He then received his card of membership. Among the Pergamene ὑμνῳδοί it was the rule that the newly-elected member should pay to each of the existing members fifteen denarii and should spend the same sum on incense in honour of the dead member whose place he was taking.

Membership was normally for life, subject to the observance of the statutes and the payment of the annual subscription. In the Attic society of ἡρωϊσταί this amounted to six drachmas, save in the case of members residing abroad, who paid but three. The clubs, however, possessed, and occasionally exercised, the right to elect honorary members.

In order to illustrate the detailed and vivid character of the epigraphical evidence, some part of which I have summarized in this lecture, let me read you a literal translation of a long and perfectly preserved text,[27] dated shortly before 178 A.D., containing an extract from the minutes of the Attic society of Iobacchi and a complete copy of its revised statutes.

"To good luck. In the archonship of Arrius Epaphroditus, on the eighth day of the month Elaphebolion, a meeting was convened for the first time by the priest who had been nominated by Aurelius Nicomachus, who had served as vice-priest for seventeen years and as priest for twenty-three years and had in his lifetime resigned his position, for the honour and glory of the Bacchic Society, in favour of the most excellent Claudius Herodes."

Nichomacus, then, having served the Society, as Vice-President and then as President, for forty years, appoints as his successor in the presidency Herodes, whom we may probably identify with Herodes Atticus, the most distinguished Athenian citizen of that day. His first official act is to nominate the outgoing President as Vice-President. The inscription continues thus:

"Nicomachus, nominated by Herodes as vice-priest, read aloud the statutes drawn up by the ex-priests Chrysippus and Dionysius, and after the priest and the arch-bacchus and the patron had expressed their approval there were shouts of 'These are what we always observe,' 'Hurrah for the priest!', 'Revive the statutes: you ought to,' 'Long life to the Bacchic Society, and good order!', 'Engrave the statutes,' 'Put the question.' The priest then said: 'Since my colleagues and I and all of you agree, we shall put the question as you demand.' Then the chairman, Rufus son of Aphrodisius, put the question: 'Whoever wishes the statutes which have been read to be ratified and engraved on a column will raise his hand.' All hands were raised. There were shouts of 'Long life to the most excellent priest Herodes!', 'Now you are in fortune: now we are the first of all Bacchic Societies,' 'Hurrah for the vice-priest!', 'Let the column be made!' The vice-priest said: 'The column shall rest upon the pillar, and the statutes shall be engraved; the officers will take care to prevent any infringement of them.'"

Then follows the text of the statutes thus ratified, in these terms.

"No one may be an Iobacchus unless he first lodge with the priest the usual notice of candidature and be approved by a vote of the Iobacchi as being clearly a worthy and suitable member of the Bacchic Society. The entrance-fee shall be fifty denarii and a libation for one who is not the son of a member, while the sons of members shall lodge a similar notice and pay, in addition to twenty-five denarii, half the usual subscription until the attainment of puberty. The Iobacchi shall meet on the ninth of each month and on the anniversary of its foundation and on the festivals of Bacchus and on any extraordinary feast of the god, and each member shall take part in word or act or honourable deed, paying the fixed monthly contribution for the wine. If he fail to pay, he shall be excluded from the gathering and this exclusion shall be enforced by those whose names are recorded in the decree, save in case of absence from home or mourning or illness or if he who is to be admitted to the gathering was under some strong compulsion, of which the priests are to judge.[28] And if the brother of an Iobacchus enter the Society after approval by vote, he shall pay fifty denarii; but if any acolyte living outside pay the sums due to the gods and to the Bacchic Society, he shall be an Iobacchus together with his father, sharing with his father in a single libation. When anyone has lodged his application and has been approved by vote, the priest shall hand him a letter stating that he is an Iobacchus, but not until he has first paid to the priest his entrance fee, and in the letter the priest shall cause to be entered the sums paid under one head or another. No one may either sing or create a disturbance or applaud at the gathering, but each shall say and act his allotted part with all good order and quietness under the direction of the priest or the arch-bacchus. No Iobacchus who has not paid his contributions for the monthly and anniversary meetings shall enter the gathering until the priests have decided either that he must pay or that he may be admitted.[29] If anyone start a fight or be found acting disorderly or occupying the seat of any other member or using insulting or abusive language to anyone, the person so abused or insulted shall produce two of the Iobacchi to state upon oath that they heard him insulted or abused, and he who was guilty of the insult or abuse shall pay to the Society twenty-five light drachmas, or he who was responsible for the fight shall pay the same sum of twenty-five drachmas, on pain of exclusion from the meetings of the Iobacchi until they make payment. And if anyone come to blows, he who has been struck shall lodge a written statement with the priest or the vice-priest, and he shall without fail convene a general meeting, and the Iobacchi shall decide the question by vote under the presidency of the priest, and the penalty shall be exclusion for a period to be determined and a fine not exceeding twenty-five silver denarii. And the same punishment shall be imposed also on one who, having been struck, fails to seek redress with the priest or the arch-bacchus but has brought a charge before the public courts. And the same punishment shall be imposed upon the orderly officer ($εὔκοσμος$) if he failed to eject those who were fighting. And if any of the Iobacchi, knowing that a general meeting ought to be convened for this purpose, fail to attend, he shall pay to the Society fifty light drachmas, and if he fail to pay on demand, the treasurer shall have power to prevent him from entering the

Bacchic Society until he pay. And if any of those who enter fail to pay the entrance-fee to the priest or to the vice-priest, he shall be excluded from the banquet until he does pay, and the money shall be exacted in whatsoever way the priest may order. And no one shall deliver a speech without the leave of the priest or of the vice-priest on pain of being liable to a fine of thirty light drachmas to the Society. The priest shall perform the customary services at the meeting and the anniversary in proper style, and shall set before the meeting the drink-offering for the return of Bacchus (τὰ καταγώγια) and pronounce the sermon, which Nicomachus the ex-priest inaugurated as an act of public spirit. And the arch-bacchus shall offer the sacrifice to the god and shall set forth the drink-offering on each tenth day of the month Elaphebolion. And when portions are distributed, let them be taken by the priest, vice-priest, arch-bacchus, treasurer, bucolicus, Dionysus, Core, Palaemon, Aphrodite and Proteurythmus[30]; and let these names be apportioned by lot among all the members. And if any of the Iobacchi receive any legacy or honour or appointment, he shall set before the Iobacchi a drink-offering corresponding to the appointment,—marriage, birth, Choes, coming of age (ἐφηβεία), citizen-status, the office of wand-bearer, councillor, president of the games, Panhellen, elder, thesmothetes, or any magistracy whatsoever, the appointment as συνθύτης or as justice of the peace, the title of ἱερονείκης, or any other promotion attained by any Iobacchus. The orderly officer shall be chosen by lot or appointed by the priest, and he shall bear the thyrsus of the god to him who is disorderly or creates a disturbance. And anyone beside whom the thyrsus is laid shall, with the approval of the priest or of the arch-bacchus, leave the banqueting-hall: but if he disobey, the ' horses ' who shall be appointed by the priests shall take him up and put him outside the front door and he shall be liable to the punishment inflicted upon those who fight. The Iobacchi shall elect a treasurer by ballot for a term of two years, and he shall take over all the property of the Bacchic Society in accordance with an inventory, and shall likewise hand it over to his successor as treasurer. And he shall provide out of his own pocket the oil for the lights[31] on each ninth day of the month and on the anniversary and at the assembly and on all the customary days of the god and on those days when legacies or honours or appointments are celebrated. And he shall, if he wish, appoint a secretary at his own risk, and he shall be allowed the treasurer's drink-offering and shall be free from the payment of subscriptions for the two years. And if any Iobacchus die, a wreath shall be provided in his honour not exceeding five denarii in value, and a single jar of wine shall be set before those who have attended the funeral; but anyone who has not attended may not partake of the wine."

A curious medley this,—religion, drama, good-fellowship, banqueting ! Yet how many traits in this description and in other records of the ancient societies find their counterparts in the medieval guilds !

What, then, did the Greek societies do for their members ? They afforded them, as we have seen, opportunities of common worship, the enjoyment of social intercourse and, in some cases at least, the satisfaction of attaining prominence and holding office. Further, the Greek club promoted among its members a brotherly spirit and mutual aid in time of difficulty : all the Iobacchi joined in celebrating any joyous occasion in the life of any member, and the statutes of an Attic θίασος provide that, if any member suffer wrong, all are to render assistance.[32] That this is a mere empty phrase I cannot believe, and when Poland lays stress on the very small number of recorded cases of such help,[33] I would reply that the assistance given was hardly likely to be commemorated by inscriptions, which are our sole source of information on this topic, and that the unquestionable popularity of clubs throughout the Greek world indicates that, for one reason or another, it was worth while to become a member.

But the societies did not content themselves with providing for their living members ; many of them also paid honours to the dead.[34] Some possessed burying-places of their own, but more frequently the tombstone alone was furnished from the funds of the society. Further, the association often took part in the funeral of a deceased member and in its attendant religious ceremonies, and in some cases secured his recognition as a " hero." Indeed, the main, or even the sole, object of some societies was to guarantee the due performance of the heroic cult of the dead. And so the bodies of which we have spoken not only bound together men and women, citizens and aliens, slaves and free in a common activity and a common loyalty during life ; they also helped, by the honours paid to their dead, to foster the conception of a still wider unity, in which the living and the dead were one.

NOTES ON LECTURE III

[1] L. Mitteis and U. Wilcken, *Grundzüge und Chrestomathie der Papyruskunde*, i. (1). 121 f. ; M. San Nicolò, *Ägyptisches Vereinswesen zur Zeit der Ptolemäer und Römer*, Munich, 1913 ff.

[2] See the list given in Poland, *Geschichte* (*infra*, note 6), 548 ff. ; some additions are made *ibid.* 545 ff. and in Lübker's *Reallexikon*,[8] 1098 f. The laws and decrees of the Attic societies are collected in *I.G.* ii.[2] 1249—1369. A selection of guild-records, *S.I.G.* 1095—1120.

[3] A. Stöckle, *Spätrömische und byzantinische Zünfte* (*Klio*, Beiheft ix), Leipzig, 1911.

[4] P. Foucart, *Des associations religieuses chez les Grecs*, Paris, 1873.

[5] E. Ziebarth, *Das griechische Vereinswesen*, Leipzig, 1896.

[6] F. Poland, *Geschichte des griechischen Vereinswesens*, Leipzig, 1909. To this great work I owe much of the material surveyed in this lecture.

[7] But see Poland, *op. cit.* 514 ff. The associations of the Bosporan kingdom are discussed in E. H. Minns, *Scythians and Greeks*, 620 ff.

[8] *Digest*, xlvii. 22. 4. Cf. M. Radin, *The Legislation of the Greeks and Romans on Corporations*, 36 ff.

[9] iii. 82.

[10] viii. 54. 4, 65.

[11] *Pol.* i. 1253 a 2 ; cf. *Eth.* i. 1097 b 11.

[12] Poland, *op. cit.* 8 ff.

[13] *Ibid.* 16 ff.

[14] *Ibid.* 28 ff.
[15] *Ibid.* 158 ff.
[16] *Ibid.* 33 ff.
[17] *Ibid.* 168 ff.
[18] *Eth.* viii. 1160 *a* 10 ff.
[19] Poland, *op. cit.* 106 ff.
[20] *Protagoras*, 311b.
[21] L. Robert, *Rev. Phil.* 1929, 136 f.
[22] C. Picard, *L'établissement des Poseidoniastes de Bérytos* (*Exploration archéologique de Délos*, vi), Paris, 1921.
[23] *Anatolian Studies presented to W. M. Ramsay*, 27ff.
[24] *Ibid.* 30, 46.
[25] Poland, *op. cit.* 282 ff.
[26] *I.G.* ii.^{2} 1365, 1366.
[27] *I.G.* ii.^{2} 1368. For a fuller bibliography see M. N. Tod, *Cl. Qu.* xxiii. 1, to which add J. Zingerle, *Jahreshefte*, xxiv. Beiblatt, 125 ff.
[28] Cf. Tod, *op. cit.* 2 ff.
[29] Cf. Tod, *op. cit.* 1 f.
[30] For this being see E. Maass, *Orpheus*, 62 ff.
[31] Cf. J. Zingerle, *op. cit.*
[32] M. N. Tod, *British School Annual*, xiii. 328 ff.
[33] Poland, *op. cit.* 502.
[34] *Ibid.* 503 ff.